POETRY MONSTERS

Creature Comforts

Edited By Jenni Harrison

First published in Great Britain in 2020 by:

YoungWriters®
Est. 1991

Young Writers
Remus House
Coltsfoot Drive
Peterborough
PE2 9BF
Telephone: 01733 890066
Website: www.youngwriters.co.uk

All Rights Reserved
Book Design by Ashley Janson
© Copyright Contributors 2019
Softback ISBN 978-1-83928-740-4

Printed and bound in the UK by BookPrintingUK
Website: www.bookprintinguk.com
YB0431H

FOREWORD

Hello Reader!

For our latest poetry competition we sent out funky and vibrant worksheets for primary school pupils to fill in and create their very own poem about fiendish fiends and crazy creatures. I got to read them and guess what? They were **roarsome**!

The pupils were able to read our example poems and use the fun-filled free resources to help bring their imaginations to life, and the result is pages **oozing** with exciting poetic tales. From friendly monsters to mean monsters, from bumps in the night to **rip-roaring** adventures, these pupils have excelled themselves, and now have the joy of seeing their work in print!

Here at Young Writers we love nothing more than poetry and creativity. We aim to encourage children to put pen to paper to inspire a love of the written word and explore their own unique worlds of creativity. We'd like to congratulate all of the aspiring authors that have created this book of **monstrous mayhem** and we know that these poems will be enjoyed for years to come. So, dive on in and submerge yourself in all things furry and fearsome (and perhaps check under the bed!).

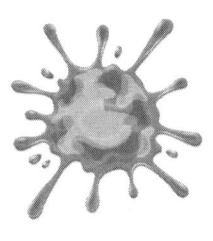

CONTENTS

Independent Entries

Alex   1

Broadacre Primary School, Hull

Isla Stevens (10)   2

Crazies Hill CE Primary School, Wargrave

Fox Drake (7)   3
Gweneira Green (8)   4
Declan Jay Mulcahy (7)   6
Robert Morane-Griffiths (8)   7
Charlie David Stollery (8)   8

Emsworth Primary School, Emsworth

Alaina Brodie (7)   9
Aidan Gosling (7)   10
Ronnie Seath (7)   11
Oliver Pengelly (7)   12
Mia Du-val (7)   13
Amber Rudman (7)   14
Josie Humphrey (7)   15
Ivy Rose McGowan (7)   16
Tullulah Creamer (7)   17
Maggie Rose Robinson (7)   18
Rowan Hicks (7)   19
Finley Lewis (8)   20
Jaden Chilaka (8)   21
George Denby (6)   22
Isla Boddington   23
Max Wild (7)   24
Jamie   25

Mylo Boxall   26
Eleanor Sowerby   27
Bethany Gosling (6)   28
Freddie Hines (8)   29
Kaan Hastekin (7)   30
Paige Rayner (7)   31
Dylan Shale (6)   32
Leila-Rose Waters (7)   33
Jack Howard (6)   34
Millie Sparrow (7)   35
Evie Rose Chatfield (7)   36
Oliver Pook (8)   37
Freddie Broughton (7)   38
Alexander Large (6)   39
Mikey Babb (7)   40
Idris Arthur (7)   41
Joshua Gallivan (7)   42
Emma Jones (7)   43
Harrison Sopp (6)   44
Sebby Haskell (7)   45
Zachary Martin (7)   46
Scarlett Ella Louise Linehan (7)   47
Charles Porter   48
Freya Edwards (6)   49
Daisy May Owusu (8)   50
Finn George Hyde (7)   51
Charley Harmer   52
Kelvin Abbey   53
Faith Marshall (7)   54
Anton Linto (6)   55
Ella Pearson (8)   56
Noah Clift (7)   57
Imogen Frost (7)   58
Tallia Hyam-Dunn (7)   59
Jayden Harris (6)   60

Sean Sebastian D'Costa (6)	61
Maisie Bell	62
Grace Etherington (5)	63
Harrison O'Nions (5)	64
James Silk (6)	65
George Elliott Butt (6)	66
Jack Stratton (6)	67
Aimee	68
Freya Chapman (5)	69
Daisy Drew (6)	70
Isabella Grace Hyde (5)	71
Emily Barrable	72
Elysia Sienna Kudhail Cross (6)	73
Zara Haskell (5)	74
Isla Lewis (5)	75
Daisy-Lyn Berwick (5)	76
Violet Elsie May Linehan (5)	77
Vinnie Dean Cooper (6)	78
Ava Du-val (5)	79
Olly	80
William Sowerby	81

Holy Trinity School & Sixth Form Centre, Kidderminster

Gabriella Corneby (10)	82
Holly Jones (9)	84
Coco Paveley (9)	86
Jacob Cutler (10)	88
Lia Chance (11)	90
Erin Lannin (9)	91
Phoebe Oldnall (9)	92
Edward Joseph Chandler (9)	94
Zubaida Khatun (10)	95
Seren Turley (9)	96
Ruby Jones (9)	97
Imogen Forsyth-Ball (10)	98
Josh Brooke (9)	99
Rosie Bryant (10)	100
Leila Miah (9)	101
Grace King (11)	102
Megan Bushell (10)	103
Lucy Gibbons (10)	104
Ellen Taylor-O'Sullivan (9)	105

Cara Moore (9)	106
Martha Crump (9)	107
Maddison Rose Fuell (10)	108
Emilia Lane (9)	109
Molly Vaughan (9)	110
Bethany Clarke (9)	111
Daisy Noake (10)	112
Hunnie Primrose Morris (9)	113
Mia Bowen (10)	114
Jalen Macnamara-Sharma (9)	115
Daniel Wilkins (9)	116
Isabelle Lowe (10)	117
Ellie Burgess (9)	118
Reggie Preece (9)	119
Archie Holmes (9)	120
Jude James Foster (9)	121
Amelia Williams (10)	122

Little Snoring Primary School, Little Snoring

Daisy Martha Bailey (11)	123
Emily Margetson (11)	124
Callum Lovick	125
Jack Edwards (9)	126
Jack Leggett	127
Kayley Rollins	128
Jake Raymond Stearman (9)	129
Mark Danby	130
Lucas Wick	131

Pilling St John's CE School, Pilling

Poppy Phillpotts (9)	132
Hannah Wilson (10)	134
Elizabeth Hill (10)	135

Stalham Academy, Stalham

Geno Gamble (10)	136
Isla Smithson (9)	137

Stanton Road Primary School, Bebington

Olivia Kelly (10)	138
Elodie Casey (10)	140
Louie Jones (10)	142
Billy (10)	144
Bethan Barnes (10)	145
Luke Brockway (10)	146
Charlie Jeakins (10)	147
Olivia Hanrahan (10)	148
Fenja Doolan (10)	149
Eva Phillips (10)	150
Douglas Waters (10)	151
Thomas Harris (10)	152
Daniel Skinner (11)	153
Maya Khan (10)	154
Calum Smith (10)	155
Alice Matchett (10)	156
Elly Noone (11)	157
Rosie Mae Higginson (10)	158

THE POEMS

Sloppy Slimer

Plated, sharp tusks,
Flaps wavy wings,
Dangerous, slippery spikes,
Soft, cuddly fur.

Alex

Monster House

I can see slimy trails on the floor,
I can hear my creaky wardrobe door,
I can hear fear-filled growls coming from under my bed,
I usually jump and bump my head.

The dark night sky feels like it is touching me,
Oh no, what is that on my knee?
It looks like a claw,
Oh no, it has run behind my door.

I muster the strength to get out of my covers,
Hoping not to serve the others,
I look behind my door,
And it's gone under the floor.

I fear I will never know what visits me at night,
I guess I have to live in fright!

Isla Stevens (10)
Broadacre Primary School, Hull

The Shadow Man Turns Good

Long ago in a dead, deep wood,
Lived a little monster called Black Eye,
Black Eye was silly and shy,
Compared to his dad, he was not very good.

One night, Black Eye's dad robbed the bank,
He jumped through the window,
He crept on the floor,
Till he got to the door,
But one of the guards spotted him, and shot him to the floor,
Once he was in prison he called his son,
And his son said, "I will be there soon,"
He ran and met a baboon.

The baboon and boy ran through the door,
There his dad was, he was sure,
Black Eye's dad looked at the baboon,
And his red eye turned good.

Fox Drake (7)
Crazies Hill CE Primary School, Wargrave

Bang Then Death

In the lonely, dark forest,
Not far from the ocean,
Lived a sad monster.
He had devil horns and a devil tail.
He had no friends,
His parents didn't even like him.
His name was Tim
And he lived in a colossal garbage bin.

One day, he saw a fluffy, pink and blue monster.
She had a dog the colour of a bog.
He turned around, jumped in the water and nearly drowned.
The pink and blue monster told him to link arms,
She pulled him up and out.

As they lay across the sand, he took her hand.
Up jumped Baby Shark, the bog dog,
And barked and barked.
As they ran, they heard a bang.
She shouted, "Stan!"
But no reply.

As they ran back, she cried and cried.
The bang had killed Stan.
As they tried to find the sharpest stone,
They succeeded and killed themselves.
Death had taken over.

Gweneira Green (8)
Crazies Hill CE Primary School, Wargrave

Monster And His Friend

Monster lived across the sea,
He wanted to fly to England, like a bee.

As soon as he got there, he made some friends,
One was called Declan who had very big hands.

When a bully called Declan some horrible names,
The monster growled and chased him down the lanes.

Declan was happy, they were such great friends,
This is how the story ends.

Declan Jay Mulcahy (7)
Crazies Hill CE Primary School, Wargrave

The Shadow

I come in peace, to talk not fight.
But sometimes I have to, all day and night.
I come for the shadow-beast of flight.

It's said to be strong, and dark to the eye.
It came to the village when the storm was at an end,
I fought it, I fought it, it doesn't make a good friend.

Robert Morane-Griffiths (8)
Crazies Hill CE Primary School, Wargrave

Monster Dog

Monster Dog was a criminal who would rob banks.
He carried a knife in his hand.
He had 1,000 hands and 10,000 eyes.
He shouted very loud, "Give me all of the money!"
They ran about.
The police in their police car came fast,
The police went to arrest the monster.

Charlie David Stollery (8)
Crazies Hill CE Primary School, Wargrave

My Monster

Her teeth are as sharp as a shark's teeth,
Her bites are as poisonous as a rattlesnake's,
Her horns are as spiky as a hedgehog's back,
Her roar is as loud as booming thunder,
Her jaw is strong enough to crush a bus,
Her toes are as rotten as a garbage bin,
She is as tall as the Eiffel Tower,
She is as excited as a puppy,
Her teeth are as sharp as a knife,
Her spikes are as sharp as a cactus,
Her fur is as fluffy as a cloud,
Her jaw is sharp enough to crush a bus,
She is as colourful as a rainbow!

Alaina Brodie (7)
Emsworth Primary School, Emsworth

Cyclopacous

Cyclopacous has a spear-like tail,
With some vicious nails on his wings,
There's lots of blood dripping like string,
I hope you meet him because he does some nasty things.
This monster will give you a fright,
And he'll make a pie and squeeze you in tight.

His lots of legs make him fast,
And that means he's super advanced,
He'll never, ever dance.
Cyclopacous, with his glowing bright eyes,
He can hypnotise you and make you into one of him,
But you have never known that he is super slim.

Aidan Gosling (7)
Emsworth Primary School, Emsworth

Spiky Scary, Sneaky, Scary, Spiky

Bouncy like an enormous trampoline,
Bright, colossal ears,
As bad as a robber,
The big, scary monster is enormous, like a giraffe,
He is big, bad and scary,
Big, spiky monster, gliding like a queen,
He is bouncing around the city,
Teeth as sharp as a crocodile's,
Legs as long as a giraffe's,
Antennae as tall as a giraffe,
He wishes he has friends,
But he always has to be alone, he says,
He is a big monster,
His name is Spiky Scary,
And he is sometimes nice,
Sometimes not nice.

Ronnie Seath (7)
Emsworth Primary School, Emsworth

Sharp-Eyed Flinn

Sharp-Eyed Flinn sits on the shelf,
He's looking in your sweet tin,
He's very menacing, with ten eyes,
And, if you don't watch out, children,
You'll be in for a surprise!

He comes out at night, looking rather dim,
He sneaks into your sweet tin,
Beware children, but don't be worried about Sharp-Eyed Flinn,
He also gives you a fright,
He is as frightening as a lion (or a tiger),
He can fly as fast as a peregrine falcon.

Oliver Pengelly (7)
Emsworth Primary School, Emsworth

Hairy Scary

Hairy Scary has a spiky tail,
An orange stomach and a glowing nail,
He's menacing and grizzly,
With a toothy grin,
A bulbous, red nose and four green spikes on his chin.
Children beware!
He loves a good scare,
Hiding in the cloakroom, lurking in the shadows,
Always looking for the best place,
Slinking under your window, close your curtains,
Turn off the light,
Find a good place to hide,
It's your turn to give him a fright!

Mia Du-val (7)
Emsworth Primary School, Emsworth

Meeting People On Earth

Hi, I'm Mr Toby Bob Junior,
I like to make friends with children,
And I fly around and meet new people on Earth.
I also sail on a boat,
And I feel the fish,
And they gently swim in the water,
Slowly flipping and darting,
And I start feeding the fish while they're flipping in the water and gobbling.
And one was different to all the other fish,
It was called a pufferfish,
It puffed and it flipped.

Amber Rudman (7)
Emsworth Primary School, Emsworth

Scary Harry

Scary Harry scares himself as well as you,
He dribbles on you, he's a dribbly thing,
He sleeps with you when you are sleeping,
He also steals your money,
He smells you at the same time as dribbling on you,
His bubbling stomach is full of your toys and teddies,
He has a sharp, spiky tail that will hurt you,
So beware, just in case he comes, tidy your room,
So he doesn't eat them!

Josie Humphrey (7)
Emsworth Primary School, Emsworth

Gooey

Gooey is as patched-up as a blanket,
Gooey is as greedy as a lion,
She's as big as a giant,
Gooey has huge eyes like a football,
Gooey is as shiny as a pin,
Gooey is as cute as a kitten,
Gooey is as purple as a flower,
Gooey is as mean as a bully,
Gooey is as dark as a bat,
Gooey has claws like a lion,
Gooey's ears are like ovals,
Watch out, Gooey's about!

Ivy Rose McGowan (7)
Emsworth Primary School, Emsworth

Sparkles

Sparkles is as fluffy as a cloud,
Sparkles has a red, fluffy hat,
As fluffy as a teddy,
Sparkles has a spiky tail,
And it is as spiky as a nail,
Sparkles has a red Christmas hat,
It is as fluffy as a cloud,
Sparkles has spiky teeth,
Sparkles has a monster, cheeky laugh,
Sparkles has a red hat,
Sparkles has a funny laugh,
Sparkles has a funny friend.

Tullulah Creamer (7)
Emsworth Primary School, Emsworth

Dribbling-Dan

Drip, drip, drip,
While gross drool drops from his mouth,
Rumbles, like a volcano is about to erupt,
Seven eyes blink at one time,
Like one will pop out,
Deadly spikes, like they could kill with one touch,
Fluffy as a teddy bear,
Yellow like the sun and as orange as an orange,
Red blood drips from his mouth,
Blue eyes are as blue as the sea.

Maggie Rose Robinson (7)
Emsworth Primary School, Emsworth

Hammer Head

His head reaches higher than the clouds,
He is as tall as the Eiffel Tower,
His roar is louder than booming thunder,
His bite is strong enough to crush a bus,
His teeth are as sharp as a knife,
His legs are like tree trunks,
When he stomps on the ground, it causes an earthquake,
He can flatten buildings with his head,
His blue eyes are like the ocean.

Rowan Hicks (7)
Emsworth Primary School, Emsworth

Smily Seb

Bang, bang, bang,
As he hit the floor,
Ten colourful eyes are staring carefully,
Mammoth arms, his hands on the steering wheel,
About to start the colossal race,
A huge, rumbling tummy is ready to eat,
A round, yellow face is searching for people,
Points that poke people,
He is as hungry as one million sharks.

Finley Lewis (8)
Emsworth Primary School, Emsworth

Hide-And-Seek

When night comes,
The beast will come,
Seek everyone with a game of hide-and-seek,
Nobody peek,
Or you'll be his meat,
He'll eat you for breakfast, lunch or dinner,
He's as thick as a cloud,
If you weigh him you'll be proud,
You can't attack him at all,
Come at him, you'll have a brawl.

Jaden Chilaka (8)
Emsworth Primary School, Emsworth

Stripy

Stripy is as orange and green as a colourful rug,
And he has feet as big as an elephant's foot,
And he is an orange spotty monster,
And he has arms as small as a rat,
And teeth as sharp as a shark's,
Because he has lots of predators,
He's very strong,
He will smash your house down!
Do not go near him.

George Denby (6)
Emsworth Primary School, Emsworth

Purple Poem

Swish, swish, swish,
Goes Purple Poem's tail,
As colourful as a rainbow,
As purple as a plum,
Stomp, stomp,
Go his feet,
He is as hungry as a lion,
He has sharp teeth like a giant shark's teeth,
He has spikes as sharp as the Gruffalo's,
He has an eye as large as the moon.

Isla Boddington
Emsworth Primary School, Emsworth

Hairy Wairy

Hairy Wairy is very scary,
He sneaks through the air,
So children, beware,
He steals your hair in the night,
And puts them in a hairy, scary bag,
He turns himself into a hairy, scary monster,
So, kids,
Maybe one night you could scare Hairy Wairy,
And he will stay at home and never come out.

Max Wild (7)
Emsworth Primary School, Emsworth

Robot Slimer

Splurge! go his small, but deadly, slime-blasters,
Scary claws killing people instantly,
Slimy slime-blasters sliming people for a feast,
Deadly spikes glueing everything to him,
Elongating arms reach for the kill,
Killer shark's mouth, chomping everything,
Claws as scary as a skeleton.

Jamie
Emsworth Primary School, Emsworth

Ball Of Hunger

Pitter-patter, pitter-patter,
His scuttling feet, hastily,
Five-mile tongue,
Grabs anything in its way,
Flower hands, in the winter they disappear,
Regrow over summer,
Curly, twirly horns,
Crunch crunch,
Go his razor-sharp teeth,
Eyes that hunt for anything.

Mylo Boxall
Emsworth Primary School, Emsworth

Colour Clover

Squeak, squeak as she talks,
Her small, cold paws rest on the wooden flooring,
One slimy, yellow eye watching,
Her orangey-yellow fur is as fluffy as a kitten,
Clover's bow swishes in the wind,
Two colourful antennae stick up as she listens,
Colour Clover is as good as a puppy.

Eleanor Sowerby
Emsworth Primary School, Emsworth

My Monster

His spikes are as sharp as a cactus,
His toes are as smelly as a garbage bin,
His legs are like tree trunks,
He is as strong as a shire horse,
He is as tall as the CN Tower, in Canada,
He is as stripy as a zebra,
He is as colourful as a rainbow,
His smile is as happy as a puppy.

Bethany Gosling (6)
Emsworth Primary School, Emsworth

Green Messy

Green Messy has sharp spikes on his back,
A giant eye and some round spots,
And a sticky tongue.
Green Messy has a menacing smile,
With two long, pointed ears.
He runs, jumps, flips, through the jungle,
Yeah,
And if you see him, be careful,
Because he might tread on you!

Freddie Hines (8)
Emsworth Primary School, Emsworth

Bossy Bob

Bossy Bob has a spiky tail,
He likes to party all day long,
He likes to creep around at night,
Bossy Bob likes to dance,
And he likes to shake his pants,
He likes to show off his fur,
As he stabs with his horns,
Bossy Bob has a black belly,
And he also has orange horns.

Kaan Hastekin (7)
Emsworth Primary School, Emsworth

Stripy Stacy

Pft goes her mouth as she licks her lips,
An eye dripping blood,
Stripes changed quickly,
Deadly spikes, silently resting,
Quietly her eyes swoosh around,
Blood is dripping rapidly out of her mouth,
One deadly eye, gleaming brightly,
As fierce as a lion roaring.

Paige Rayner (7)
Emsworth Primary School, Emsworth

My Monster

He is as tall as the Eiffel Tower,
His bite is as poisonous as a rattlesnake's,
His legs are like tree trunks,
His fur is as fluffy as a cloud,
His toenails are as rotten as a garbage bin,
His growl is as loud as a fighter jet,
His roar is as loud as booming thunder.

Dylan Shale (6)
Emsworth Primary School, Emsworth

Moonee Moo

Moonee Moo is sleepy,
When he sleeps, children beware,
Moonee Moo is a very small monster,
With a crescent moon on his head,
He has giant, floating eyes,
And tiny arms and legs,
An enormous glowing smile with tiny braces,
And glittering shoes with sparkling laces.

Leila-Rose Waters (7)
Emsworth Primary School, Emsworth

My Monster

His horns are as pointed as the Spinnaker Tower,
He's got more claws than all the stars in the galaxy,
His leg is as thick as a tree trunk,
He's as strong as a shire horse,
He's as tall as the Eiffel Tower,
He's as ginormous as a bucket-wheel excavator.

Jack Howard (6)
Emsworth Primary School, Emsworth

Hairy Scary

Hairy Scary has sharp claws,
He loves to dance and he goes to parties all day long,
He is a friendly monster,
He knocks at your door and gives you party sweets,
And smiles at everyone he meets,
He might look scary,
But don't worry, he's really nice.

Millie Sparrow (7)
Emsworth Primary School, Emsworth

Devil Wish

My monster has pigtails,
My monster has little eyes,
My monster has pointy horns that can stab,
My monster has sharp yellow teeth,
My monster has rings on her fingers,
My monster has stinky feet,
My monster has a sword,
My monster has a round body.

Evie Rose Chatfield (7)
Emsworth Primary School, Emsworth

Clumsy Dumsy

Sizzle, sizzle goes the volcano on his eyes,
Pft goes his boiling mouth,
Deadly spikes, cutting a tomato,
Razor-sharp teeth feasting on a lion,
Eyes hypnotising a human,
Belly rumbling as loud as thunder,
Tentacles poisoning a fish.

Oliver Pook (8)
Emsworth Primary School, Emsworth

Sneaky Peaky

Sneaky Peaky has a dark spot,
He sneaks around at night,
To give children a fright,
So beware that he doesn't peek on you.
He can become invisible,
So when that bell rings at night,
It means that Sneaky Peaky is on the move, to give that fright.

Freddie Broughton (7)
Emsworth Primary School, Emsworth

My Monster

His teeth are sharp enough to crush a bus,
His feet are hotter than the sun,
His roar is as loud as thunder,
His claws are as sharp as 1,000 darts,
He is as nasty as the nastiest goblin,
He is as gigantic as a bucket-wheel excavator.

Alexander Large (6)
Emsworth Primary School, Emsworth

Spiky Mikey

Bing, bong,
Feet stomping along,
Eyes red as lava,
Bang, bang,
Go his orange fists,
Razor-sharp teeth,
Spiky back,
Red, spotty back,
Pop, pop, goes his bottom,
Like a trumpet.

Mikey Babb (7)
Emsworth Primary School, Emsworth

Weird Mid

Weird Mid has a head in his tummy,
Tentacles as sticky as sticky mud,
Two small heads in one,
Beware, he could be anywhere,
Under your bed, on your chair,
Because he will spook you at first sight,
Like *splat!*

Idris Arthur (7)
Emsworth Primary School, Emsworth

My Big Bad Monster

He is as tall as the Eiffel Tower,
His hair is as spiky as a cactus,
His fur is as fluffy as a cloud,
His roar is as loud as booming thunder,
His jaw is strong enough to crush a bus,
His growl is as loud as a fighter jet.

Joshua Gallivan (7)
Emsworth Primary School, Emsworth

Rainbow

Rainbow is as soft as a lion's mane,
Rainbow is as funny as a joker,
Rainbow is as bubbly as a young child,
Rainbow is as rainbow-y as a child's room,
Rainbow has bright fur and eats up my worries,
Rainbow.

Emma Jones (7)
Emsworth Primary School, Emsworth

Spony

Colossal, skinny legs,
Spiky, long tail,
He's got googly eyes,
And he is the spikiest monster in the world,
He is the strongest monster you have ever seen,
But be careful, because he might eat you in the night.

Harrison Sopp (6)
Emsworth Primary School, Emsworth

Lightning Bolt

Rattle, rattle goes his floppy tail,
Scary but weird,
Steam, sizzle goes the pyramid on his head,
Beware, razor-sharp dagger,
Deadly slime runs down,
Disgraceful, devours like a headless chicken.

Sebby Haskell (7)
Emsworth Primary School, Emsworth

Cuddle

Cuddle likes to snuggle,
He sometimes gets in a muddle,
He has a spiky tail,
And he's as slow as a snail,
He has a giant eye, in the middle of his head,
Which is so big you can use it as a bed.

Zachary Martin (7)
Emsworth Primary School, Emsworth

Mystery Miner

Bang, bang,
Go her bloody legs,
Six huge tentacles grapple onto things,
Like a shooting star,
Whoosh, whoosh,
Go the monster's flaming eyes,
Colossal bangs of lightning.

Scarlett Ella Louise Linehan (7)
Emsworth Primary School, Emsworth

Zombie Sid

Stinky fumes float above Sid,
Bloody swords drip,
As he cuts his prey,
Red eyes watch everything,
Razor-sharp teeth chomp,
Six black arms grab food,
As stinky as an elephant and fossil poo!

Charles Porter
Emsworth Primary School, Emsworth

The Terrifying Beast

It has sharp claws,
And the monster has some friends,
And the monster plays with her friends,
And the monster has dinner every night,
And breakfast and lunch,
And she has scales that are green.

Freya Edwards (6)
Emsworth Primary School, Emsworth

Cutie Pie

Sss hisses as a snake hisses,
Sniff, sniff, snot falls down,
Flutter, flutter, her wings flap,
Tap, tap, feet tap,
Bam, boom, bang, as they fall asleep.

Daisy May Owusu (8)
Emsworth Primary School, Emsworth

Killer Pool Blader

Blood like fire drips from his mouth,
Strong arms like a tree,
Four swords like Chinese long swords
A dagger that shoots knives,
Spikes, covered over teeth,
Black arms like the dark.

Finn George Hyde (7)
Emsworth Primary School, Emsworth

Pink Pin

Swish, swish goes her tail in the sun,
A bright pink coat shines,
Two blue, bubbly fangs,
Four tappy paws,
Two gleaming blue eyes,
And *pat, pat* go her little paws.

Charley Harmer
Emsworth Primary School, Emsworth

Spiky

Drip, drip go his two black mouths,
Orange spikes drip painfully,
Red eyes burst with water,
Smells like a bin,
Deadly as a wild lion,
As scary as a fierce lion.

Kelvin Abbey
Emsworth Primary School, Emsworth

Bendy Is A Happy Monster

He has a purple tummy,
But he likes to eat children,
He thinks they're very tasty,
He's inky, colourful and soft inside,
But when he's hungry, you need to hide.

Faith Marshall (7)
Emsworth Primary School, Emsworth

My Monster

He is as tall as the Spinnaker Tower.
His horn is as sharp as a sword.
His eyes are as round as a drum.
His roar is as loud as a T-rex.
His stomp is as loud as an elephant.

Anton Linto (6)
Emsworth Primary School, Emsworth

Scary Hairy

Scary Hairy was hiding,
In the party,
And was very hungry for some lunch,
Which is a child,
One or two children,
The children at the party,
He ate all of them.

Ella Pearson (8)
Emsworth Primary School, Emsworth

Shorty

Stomping as loud as a rumbling volcano,
Sharp, pointy, swishy tail,
Googly, springy eyes,
Five slimy legs,
Big mouth,
Cuddly arms,
He is as loud as a lion.

Noah Clift (7)
Emsworth Primary School, Emsworth

Black Ninja

Rattle, rattle,
His whip shakes loudly,
As deadly as a hungry lion,
The spikiest ear in the world,
Sinking through the city,
Skin as smooth as a slug.

Imogen Frost (7)
Emsworth Primary School, Emsworth

Hairy Funny Monster

Super funny,
Happily making tea,
Slither, slither,
Zzzz,
Swivelling eyes,
Swish, swish, swish,
His legs stroll along.

Tallia Hyam-Dunn (7)
Emsworth Primary School, Emsworth

My Monster

His claws are as spiky as a cactus,
His fur is as black as the night sky,
He has lots of eyes, like a fly,
His growl is as loud as a fighter jet.

Jayden Harris (6)
Emsworth Primary School, Emsworth

My Monster

His claws are as sharp as a knife,
His horns are as pointed as the Spinnaker Tower,
He has lips like a spider,
His fur is as black as my hair.

Sean Sebastian D'Costa (6)
Emsworth Primary School, Emsworth

Cutie Pie

Swish, swish, tail in the wind,
Zzz, zzz, sleeping,
Splash, splash, getting muddy,
Halloween bow in her hair.

Maisie Bell
Emsworth Primary School, Emsworth

The Slopy

Has got black hair so it can camouflage in black stuff,
Has got yellow eyes so it can see well in the dark,
Has got red, sharp claws.

Grace Etherington (5)
Emsworth Primary School, Emsworth

The Zoolyon

It has forty eyes, that come off at night,
Its wings go invisible in the daytime,
Its legs are pointy,
Its claws are poisonous.

Harrison O'Nions (5)
Emsworth Primary School, Emsworth

The Scary Slug

He is like a snake,
But he has antennae,
And he has a sharp point at the end of his tail,
So don't touch the end of it.

James Silk (6)
Emsworth Primary School, Emsworth

My Monster

He is as excited as a tiny puppy,
His roar is as loud as booming thunder,
His claws are as sharp as a razor blade.

George Elliott Butt (6)
Emsworth Primary School, Emsworth

The Scary Beast

He is fierce and he has tusks,
He lives in the lava with a fire-worm,
He is friendly,
He has forty teeth.

Jack Stratton (6)
Emsworth Primary School, Emsworth

The Mushroom Monster

Sharp, sparkly scales,
Pointy, sparkly ears,
Sharp, dangerous claws,
Dangerous, pointy teeth.

Aimee
Emsworth Primary School, Emsworth

The Sea Dragon

Furry and soft like a cat,
Razor-sharp claws like a cat,
Very cute like a cat,
Gigantic ears.

Freya Chapman (5)
Emsworth Primary School, Emsworth

Toddy

It is scaly, slimy and cute,
It is a helpful monster,
It likes cuddles,
It is a kind monster.

Daisy Drew (6)
Emsworth Primary School, Emsworth

The Birthday Monster

Round eyes,
The nose is pointy,
The wings are fiery wings,
The scales look like bumpy hills

Isabella Grace Hyde (5)
Emsworth Primary School, Emsworth

Tiny

Rainbow-patterned eyes,
Legs lit up with the moon
Claws sharp as a dragon
Fur was painful

Emily Barrable
Emsworth Primary School, Emsworth

The Jolly Beast

He is kind and helpful,
He loves cuddles,
He is a happy monster,
He loves playing games.

Elysia Sienna Kudhail Cross (6)
Emsworth Primary School, Emsworth

The Jelly Beast

Furry monster fighting, stomping,
The gross, green skin glowing,
Eyes that glow in the dark.

Zara Haskell (5)
Emsworth Primary School, Emsworth

The Love Heart

Green and orange eyes,
It has a pink and stripy nose,
It is red,
Its noise is loud.

Isla Lewis (5)
Emsworth Primary School, Emsworth

The Llar Llar

Long stretchy eyes
Squishy ears,
Big long tail
Circled, long knobbly knees.

Daisy-Lyn Berwick (5)
Emsworth Primary School, Emsworth

Rose

My scales are scary
My fur is fluffy,
My tail is spiky,
My teeth are sharp.

Violet Elsie May Linehan (5)
Emsworth Primary School, Emsworth

Spiky Bob

Hungry as ten thousand sharks,
Fast as a cheetah,
He can swim ten miles.

Vinnie Dean Cooper (6)
Emsworth Primary School, Emsworth

The Love Heart Monster

Yellow ears,
Pink, googly eyes,
Purple nose,
Shiny mouth.

Ava Du-val (5)
Emsworth Primary School, Emsworth

Dangerous

Sharp claws,
Long, wiggly tail,
Sharp teeth,
Wings flap.

Olly
Emsworth Primary School, Emsworth

The Fire

It has wings,
It has sequins,
It has horns,
It has eyes.

William Sowerby
Emsworth Primary School, Emsworth

Creepy Monsters

Creepy, weepy monsters, big and small,
Some under the bed, some inside the wall.
But my creepy monster, he does behave,
My nickname for him is Dave.

Dave doesn't live under my bed or in my wall,
He lives in my cupboard and he is quite small.
He is so small, I do declare,
That sometimes I can't find him anywhere.

If he's in my cupboard, he's lost in the clothes,
The skirts, leggings and socks with no toes.
If the room is black and dark,
Soon it will light up with a spark.

And you'll see two yellow eyes,
You'll feel scared until you realise,
It's just Dave, in the dead of night,
But he's not so scary when you turn on the light.

I love my monster so creepy,
And he protects me when I'm feeling sleepy.

When I'm fast asleep and it's dead quiet,
Dave goes back to the cupboard in silence.

And then he'll go to sleep in the clothes,
The leggings, the skirts and the socks with no toes.

Gabriella Corneby (10)
Holy Trinity School & Sixth Form Centre, Kidderminster

The Monster That No One Had Seen

I have a friend that no one has seen,
He looks big and so tall and very, very mean.
He lives in my closet and comes out when it's dark,
He looks really scary, with a bite worse than his bark.
But trust me, I know, for he is my friend,
A real big softy that makes your hair stand on end.

If you were to see him you may be surprised,
The love and affection that shines through his eyes.
So, I've decided to name him and call him Fred,
He's moved out from the closet and lives under my bed.

One day when my mama was cleaning my room,
She discovered my monster and thought she was doomed.
But, to her surprise, my monster said, "Hi,"
My mama, she fainted, stared up at the sky.

I gathered him up and put him away,
Back into my closet and there he would stay.
My mama woke up, she thought she had dreamed,
But I know the truth about what she had seen.

Holly Jones (9)
Holy Trinity School & Sixth Form Centre, Kidderminster

Mr Shape-Shifter II Tries To Take Over!

O nce, there was a huge monster, with a humongous tongue,
N amed Mr Shape-Shifter II, he had:
E normous big ears and lips,

C razy hair, sticking out everywhere,
R ed eyebrow, blue eyebrow, green eyebrow and nose,
A hh! No more time for describing, he's here!
Z esty, sour lemon juice, he squeezes at us,
Y uck! Why yuck? Nevermind, we need to defeat him.

B ake him? Cook him?
I wouldn't cut him, he's got too much fat,
G oing to save the world!

M onday morning, this is so hard,
O n a Wednesday it's probably easy,
N o! He's coming closer,
S lish and a slash, I kill him,
T he crowd cheers for me,
E nd of the day, yay!
R elaxing time now.

Coco Paveley (9)
Holy Trinity School & Sixth Form Centre, Kidderminster

A Ghost With A Difference...

It is vigorous and it's vast,
Ferocious and it's fast,
Oh, the horrible mess it can cast,
The ghost that haunts my soul outdoors,
Attacks me with its feet and claws.

It wafts itself through my nose,
It curls in-between my toes,
It flew through the tunnel of my ears,
The ghost that haunts my soul outdoors,
Attacks me with its feet and claws.

It smashes my prize vase,
My plant pot, pictures and jars,
Oh, the hysteria,
The ghost that haunts my soul outdoors,
Attacks me with its feet and claws.

Now you have heard the comprehensive,
It would make you truly apprehensive,

One more description my brain has pinned,
Just between me and you, it's truly the wind.

Jacob Cutler (10)
Holy Trinity School & Sixth Form Centre, Kidderminster

Bloop

I have been with Bloop for as long as I can remember,
We met a few years ago, back in September,
I was playing in the garden, on my swing,
When I heard a knock and the doorbell ring,
I answered the door and I saw...
A box on the floor.

Inside was a creature, almost cute and really fluffy,
It looked a bit like a puppy,
Since then, Bloop has been my best friend,
And our connection has never come to an end,
Our favourite game is hide-and-seek,
When Bloop counts, he likes to peek,
His favourite spot is under the bed,
But when he gets under he always bumps his head.

Bloop's no fright,
Oh, what a night,
I wish it would never end,
I say goodnight to my furry friend.

Lia Chance (11)
Holy Trinity School & Sixth Form Centre, Kidderminster

Moggy The Marvellous Monster

In the hall where all the monsters creep and crawl,
Most people think that monsters are scary,
With big, sharp teeth and skin that's hairy,
They creep and crawl in the dark hall,
Except for Moggy, she's not scary at all!
Moggy, in fact, has got big, sharp teeth, that's true,
But her teeth would never hurt me or you,
Her eyes are kind and very green,
She's the prettiest monster you've ever seen,
She's very tall with hair that's pink,
But that's not all that you would think,
There are girls and boys that play with toys,
And they all make a lot of noise,
Moggy's never angry and cross,
Because everyone knows that she's the boss.

Erin Lannin (9)
Holy Trinity School & Sixth Form Centre, Kidderminster

Where Are You Monster Teddybear?

Monsters, monsters everywhere,
But where is Monster Teddybear?
I've looked here and there,
And everywhere.

Monsters, monsters everywhere,
Where are you Monster Teddybear?

Monsters, monsters everywhere,
But where is Monster Teddybear?
How I really care,
And care.

Monsters, monsters everywhere,
Where are you Monster Teddybear?

Monsters, monsters everywhere,
Where are you dear Teddybear?
I've looked here and there,
And everywhere.

There!
I see you Teddybear,
How much I care,
About you Monster Teddybear.

Monsters, monsters everywhere,
But you're my favourite teddy bear.

Phoebe Oldnall (9)
Holy Trinity School & Sixth Form Centre, Kidderminster

Barry

I woke up in the middle of the night to a bang!
Followed by a smash and a crash,
So downstairs I crept, while everyone else slept and slept.
The noises were getting louder and I felt my insides turn into powder.
So there I was, rooted to the spot, like a helpless baby in its cot,
Not at all feeling sleepy but the house started to sound creepy...
Snore, snore and *snore*, I listened to this noise more and more.
I jumped through to the kitchen, I saw a tiny little monster sleeping on the floor.
He had twelve cute eyes, wore human clothes and had a shark fin,
And I said, "My tiny little monster, you have made quite a din!"

Edward Joseph Chandler (9)
Holy Trinity School & Sixth Form Centre, Kidderminster

Zoo Zoo In Your Dream

In a house which is dark and gloomy,
You will find a monster in the room.
He makes a stomp as he gets near,
You wake up instantly but he's not here.

It's the Zoo Zoo Monster!
He is scary but shy and he doesn't like to be seen,
When he sees you, however, he will end up in your dream.
You will scream in fear,
Because you know he is near.

You try to escape but he never gives up.
He will catch you while you run,
But you can only escape with the rising sun.
With his eerie, skinny fingers he tries to catch you by your ear,
Unfortunately, there is nothing left you can do to end this petrifying fear.

Zubaida Khatun (10)
Holy Trinity School & Sixth Form Centre, Kidderminster

Spotty The Rainbow Monster

A monster, a monster, under my bed,
Is it real? Or is it in my head?
Do you think he needs the loo?
And if so, I bet it's a number two!

Out he comes, to play fun games,
To start, he gets to learn our names.
Is he in a playful mood
Or does he need a plate of food?

He creeps up slowly to my feet,
And starts to dance to a jiggy, jiggy beat!
I think he wants to play with me,
Or does he need a big, long wee?

And suddenly, to my surprise,
He disappears right in front of my eyes!
He's not in the wardrobe, not behind the door,
Guess where I find him… in my knicker drawer!

Seren Turley (9)
Holy Trinity School & Sixth Form Centre, Kidderminster

Fred

Me and Ted say, "Hi," to Fred,
The monster who lives at the end of my bed,
"A monster? Argh!" I hear you say,
"Don't just sit there, run away!"
But Fred's quite cute, he's vibrant green,
He's the fluffiest thing you've ever seen.

Neon orange spikes, all down his back,
Three bulbous eyes, that are beetle-black,
A long fork-like, green tail,
That would make even the bravest of parents pale!

He cuddles me, like I do Ted,
He helps me sleep when I'm in bed,
So if you see a monster too,
Don't be afraid, he might like you!

Ruby Jones (9)
Holy Trinity School & Sixth Form Centre, Kidderminster

The Little Monster

What's that noise I can hear?
Where is it coming from?
As it bangs and clatters,
I hear a scream and a little roar,
I hear my mum shout, "It's behind the door!"

I rush down to take a peek,
I look inside and there's a shriek,
A tiny figure emerges from the dust and gloom,
It tries to puff itself up like a balloon.

But this balloon pops and falls over,
As she does, the fruit bowl wobbles and topples over,
And a banana falls on her shoulder.
Here's a tiny word, "Yes, I did it, yay. Teeny yay."
But then spots me and runs away.

Imogen Forsyth-Ball (10)
Holy Trinity School & Sixth Form Centre, Kidderminster

Meeting The Monster

When I opened my wardrobe door,
I heard a swishing and a mighty roar.
I had gone to get my school uniform out,
What I saw made me scream and shout.
There was a giant lizard, as big as a kangaroo,
With scales and a long swishy tail, stood still as a statue.
My heart started to race
Until I saw a smile on the monster's face.
I looked into his big, green eyes
And he said, "I have been waiting to meet you and give you a surprise."
I screamed again when I heard his voice
And slammed the door to hide the noise.
When I re-opened the door,
The monster was no more!

Josh Brooke (9)
Holy Trinity School & Sixth Form Centre, Kidderminster

Fuzzy

I've lost my monster,
She was a big stomper,
She has big paws,
Like someone who doesn't do their chores.

I've seen one with a massive head,
I've seen one who loves to go to bed,
I've seen one who doesn't like their sport,
I've seen one who doesn't snort.

I've seen one who is like a dinosaur,
I've seen one who likes to *roar*,
I've seen one with pointy ears,
I've seen one badly in tears.

I've seen one who is soft and fuzzy,
Bang! It sounds familiar,
It sounds like my monster...

Rosie Bryant (10)
Holy Trinity School & Sixth Form Centre, Kidderminster

Monster Under My Bed

Under my bed, there's a monster called Ted,
He has one big eye and his favourite food is fabulous pie,
As you know, he lives under my bed,
He is tall and slimy, with a great big head.

You wouldn't dare to cross his path,
As he could easily have you for his snack,
When he cooks his pie, he makes a great big monster mess,
When, by accident, he falls into the swamp,
He will be covered in mud from head to toes,
He's a stinky monster with a scary face ready for a chase,
Out to spook anyone he meets,
So beware when you go to sleep.
Raah!

Leila Miah (9)
Holy Trinity School & Sixth Form Centre, Kidderminster

What Lurks Under The Bed

The crimson-red eyes search for their unsuspecting victim,
The hairy, wretched body lingers about,
The many legs scuttle about, looking for the next idiotic creature,
To venture into his lair of bloodshed.

Mother enters the creature's room,
Eddie said, "There is something under my bed."
Mother picks the creature up,
"It's only a spider," she said,
"Hi, I'm Walnut, don't be upset,
You don't need to worry about little old me,
I'm too clumsy to hurt you,
I have eight legs, you see!"

Grace King (11)
Holy Trinity School & Sixth Form Centre, Kidderminster

Gloopy The Gloop

He has big teeth, he has big jaws,
He has big feet, he has big claws.
He farts a lot but likes to play,
He wants to laugh and run all day.
He may seem funny but that is just wrong,
He has a friend called Ding Dong.

It's sometimes fun, it's sometimes bad,
But if he chooses, his name could be Fad.
He isn't that bad but he isn't that good,
But he has been my friend since childhood.
I'm his friend and he is mine,
Even if he got my card declined.
We are still pals, beyond combined,
Even by the seaside.

Megan Bushell (10)
Holy Trinity School & Sixth Form Centre, Kidderminster

Fantastic Little Fred

There is a monster, his name is Fred,
He made his dwelling upon my bed,
He hogs my pillow,
But he is so very cute,
Sometimes I scream, "You selfish little brute!"
But he likes it when I read him stories about the scary door,
So I think I can take a little bit more,
But he is so very cute,
And even has a button to mute,
But today, Fred is leaving,
And how I did some pleading,
He said we could meet once a year,
I said, "Okay, my dear,"
Now he has gone, it is so very bad,
And I am very, very sad.

Lucy Gibbons (10)
Holy Trinity School & Sixth Form Centre, Kidderminster

My Cheeky Monster

There's a monster under my bed,
My mum thinks it is all in my head.

He's blue and pink with furry bits,
I hope he does not have monster nits.

I can smell his breath when he yawns,
And he has very sharp, rusty-coloured horns.

His teeth are yellow,
And he steals my pillow.

He sneaks downstairs and drinks my milk,
And I would like to call him Ilk.

I have caught him on my dad's Xbox,
And I'm sure he has hidden all the odd socks.

He's definitely my cheeky monster!

Ellen Taylor-O'Sullivan (9)
Holy Trinity School & Sixth Form Centre, Kidderminster

Eugene The Mean

Eugene the Mean,
He eats the toes of children,
Although he's very lean,
He swims across the ocean.

His hair is as spiky as thorns,
He has skin as dark as mud,
Although he has no horns,
He still walks with a *thud*,
Juicy toes are his favourite snack,
But also fond of ears in a pack.

To get them, he would do anything,
Are you surprised he has no friends?
When he rings the bell at night, *ding dong ding*,
Off he mysteriously descends...

Cara Moore (9)
Holy Trinity School & Sixth Form Centre, Kidderminster

Child-Eating Cake

When Grandpa told me a bedtime story,
About a child-eating cake,
I thought, so gory,
This is not a story for bed,
It will leave nightmares in my head.

With fierce teeth,
And googly eyes,
Children go in tasty pies,
Thin ones, fat ones, all the time,
I love cake and cake loves me,
It doesn't happen normally.

Really, Grandpa, I'm so wrong,
I could put it in a song,
Because I realised, my mistake,
The story was about a child, eating cake.

Martha Crump (9)
Holy Trinity School & Sixth Form Centre, Kidderminster

Midnight Dreams

My monster under my bed,
Looks like a flower's head,
She keeps me safe at night,
With her glowing light.
Once, one night,
She escaped to my bin,
And got pricked by a pin.
"Ouch!" she screamed,
As it awoke me from my dream,
Something beamed out of her cloud-like fur.
When I realised this was all a blur,
I fell asleep once more,
When she bounced out of the door,
"Goodnight, I will see you again tomorrow," she whispered.

Maddison Rose Fuell (10)
Holy Trinity School & Sixth Form Centre, Kidderminster

Spat And The Fat Cat

In a dark home lived a monster called Spat,
Spat found a cat who was very, very fat.
Spat had red eyes and a sideways belly button,
that went out to the side,
If he looked in the mirror, he would have cried.
He is very silly and funny,
And he has a cute bunny.
He loved the bunny with all of his heart,
Except for when it does a big fart.
The cat ran away because of the smell of the bunny,
Spat smiled and waved because he thought it was funny.

Emilia Lane (9)
Holy Trinity School & Sixth Form Centre, Kidderminster

The Human-Eating Sock

Monster Sock, Monster Sock, as sly as a fox,
Roams through your drawers, giving a roar!
He wakes people up in the middle of the night,
By giving them a fright.
He can smell you from a mile away,
Even when you've had your bath for the day.
All you need to do is keep a look-out, or he could end up in your bed tonight,
Giving you a tiny, little fright!
P.S. This monster is on the roam and looking for you!
What will you do?

Molly Vaughan (9)
Holy Trinity School & Sixth Form Centre, Kidderminster

There's A Monster Over There

There's a monster over there,
He's sitting on my chair,
Is he a cat? Wait, no he's a rat,
His body parts stitched together,
He's oozing with goo,
What should I do?
Now he's a cow,
Should I bow?
He's leaving a long trail of poo,
Wait, if I look closer, it's just a trail of goo,
"John, are you in your room?"
"Yes," but there's a...
Silence.

Bethany Clarke (9)
Holy Trinity School & Sixth Form Centre, Kidderminster

My Monster Ed

My monster Ed,
He lives under the bed,
He likes to eat old socks,
But that might give him people-pox.

My monster Ed,
He's very fluffy too,
But he is very tired now and wants to go to bed,
But look, he hasn't been fed,
So I give him some food,
Then we go upstairs to bed.

My monster Ed,
Has now been fed,
So we both snuggle up,
And climb into bed.

Daisy Noake (10)
Holy Trinity School & Sixth Form Centre, Kidderminster

Scary Room

I was walking in a room one night,
When the sight of goo caught my sight,
When I turned around, to my delight,
I saw a little girl flying a kite.

Next to her, standing very tall,
Was Lactontin, in a very black pool,
He was sat in a pool full of goo,
Look a bit closer and you'll think it is poo.

She asked me if I wanted to play,
I said, "No not 'til day."

Hunnie Primrose Morris (9)
Holy Trinity School & Sixth Form Centre, Kidderminster

There Is Slime On My Bed

With slime for a body and a bobble for a head,
It comes into my room and slimes up onto my bed.
It ate my pet cat,
And even my brother's pet rat.
It moves like a slug,
And flies like a horrible bug.
I feel it, it's atrocious,
That thing can be quite ferocious.
One day, I am happy to say,
The thing, it flew away.
One day, I found its head,
But no slime in my bed.

Mia Bowen (10)
Holy Trinity School & Sixth Form Centre, Kidderminster

Jaws

He likes children and, if he finds you, you're the perfect treat,
Make sure you don't peep or you will be double the treat.
I heard a noise, what could it be?
I looked under the bed and it was not there,
I looked above and pulled my sheet above my head...
It was there!
Ahh!
He just had a treat,
Don't double it or you could be its feast!

Jalen Macnamara-Sharma (9)
Holy Trinity School & Sixth Form Centre, Kidderminster

Gibbley The One-Eyed Monster

Gibbley is a one-eyed monster,
He stares at you with his one multicoloured eye,
He makes children scream, run away and cry,
He ran away to a volcano nearby,
Gibbley was lonely and started to cry,
One tear, as big as the sky, fell into the erupting volcano,
Everyone cheered and clapped and said, "Hooray!"
Gibbley saved the day!

Daniel Wilkins (9)
Holy Trinity School & Sixth Form Centre, Kidderminster

Squiggle

Squiggle, Squiggle, cute and squishy,
Small and cute and squeals a lot,
Yet I can put him in a pot,
Small head, small hands, small brain,
He's kind of stupid, what a shame,
He eats my cookies,
He eats my hair,
If only he could just eat air,
I love my monster,
Small and sweet,
He was the best birthday treat.

Isabelle Lowe (10)
Holy Trinity School & Sixth Form Centre, Kidderminster

A Friendly Monster

Once there was a monster who lived under my bed,
His name was Fred,
And he was fuzzy and red,
With a great big head.
All day long we would play together,
And have all the fun in the world,
At night he would sleep under my bed,
And the heat would rise from him,
And keep me nice and warm.

Ellie Burgess (9)
Holy Trinity School & Sixth Form Centre, Kidderminster

My Friend Claws

My friend, Claws,
Is a monster, of course,
He lives in my bedroom, under the bed,
He wakes me up to get fed.
He has big jaws,
And scary claws,
I'm not scared, he is my friend,
He is big, shy and loving,
And will always look after me.
He's my best friend.

Reggie Preece (9)
Holy Trinity School & Sixth Form Centre, Kidderminster

Spots

Spots was spotty,
In the corner of my eye, Spots was always there.

Spots was spotty in the corner of my eye,
Spots was over there.

Spots was happy,
Spots was sad.

Spots was always there,
Spots was over there.

Archie Holmes (9)
Holy Trinity School & Sixth Form Centre, Kidderminster

Bobby

My monster's name is Bobby,
He lives in my living room,
I find him really funny,
As I don't know what he's going to do.

Yesterday, I walked in,
And he was pulling funny faces,
While doing up my laces.

Jude James Foster (9)
Holy Trinity School & Sixth Form Centre, Kidderminster

Monsters

M onstrous but magnificent
O val and ominous
N aughty but nice
S cary and sweet
T icklish but tough
E normous and edgy
R ed but rotten
S limy and snotty.

Amelia Williams (10)
Holy Trinity School & Sixth Form Centre, Kidderminster

Sad Brian

If you hear a creak,
Please don't run or hide,
I'm searching for a friend,
And have only just arrived.

People say I'm scary,
Which makes me lonely and sad,
When I am simply misunderstood,
And not at all mean or bad.

I can change colour,
To express different emotions,
But, most of the time, I'm blue,
Which causes much commotion.

Daisy Martha Bailey (11)
Little Snoring Primary School, Little Snoring

Blobby

Thump, thump, thump, as he blobs through the door,
Sneaks into the kitchen to raid my fridge,
My eyes flicker open, to hear a strange sound,
But when I got downstairs there was nothing around.

I took a walk down a sunny lane,
When he ran past a house and jumped onto the windowpane,
He waved goodbye and wagged his tail,
And, after that, I never saw him again.

Emily Margetson (11)
Little Snoring Primary School, Little Snoring

Huge-Mouth Gary

Huge-Mouth Gary is bloodthirsty and terrifying to see,
With black fur, like the night, so you don't see him coming,
He has horns covered in sparkly diamonds,
Fierce blue and green scales all over his face,
His menacing tongue is all slimy,
And his teeth are orange and stand out,
His breath smells like cabbage and will make you feel sick.

Callum Lovick
Little Snoring Primary School, Little Snoring

Cosmos

He is black as the night,
His skin glows bright,
He makes you sleepy,
So he can sneak into your fridge.

He is mischevious and cranky,
And his mechanical body is clanky,
He loves stuffing his face,
With delicious chocolate.

Jack Edwards (9)
Little Snoring Primary School, Little Snoring

Jimbo The Blob

Jimbo the blob monster,
Has smooth, slimy skin,
He will squeeze through small cracks,
And make a huge din.

He likes to change colour,
Always wins hide-and-seek,
And raids through your fridge,
When you are asleep.

Jack Leggett
Little Snoring Primary School, Little Snoring

Boom!

He is small and spotty,
With sharp, red horns,
He loves crashing parties,
And acts up a storm.

He is devious and mischievous,
And jumps out when you sleep,
He sets off stink bombs,
When you sit down to eat.

Kayley Rollins
Little Snoring Primary School, Little Snoring

Splugton

I may look hairy,
Disgusting and small,
But trust me,
I'm not to be messed with at all.

I'm poisonous and scary,
With grips for my toes,
I'm as quick as a flash,
And have a slime-cannon nose.

Jake Raymond Stearman (9)
Little Snoring Primary School, Little Snoring

Gengar

His ghost-like body is dark, devil-red,
He has sharp claws and teeth,
And a poisonous tongue.

He climbs up onto your bed,
In the middle of the night,
And bites his venom into your skin.

Mark Danby
Little Snoring Primary School, Little Snoring

Giant Mouth Bob

He has spikes all down his legs,
And he has poisonous fangs,
He sneaks into fridges,
When people are sleeping.

Lucas Wick
Little Snoring Primary School, Little Snoring

The Monsters In Plain Sight

Open the door and shut it quickly,
Because what is behind will truly frighten,
But I do not care.
If they escape, they will venture far and near,
Over hills and mountains,
Across rivers and oceans,
Petrifying many people, who are not so courageous.
Careful of the creatures,
With their sharp horns and rigid teeth,
Blowing fire out of their huge and disgusting-looking mouths,
With fluffy coats come some,
And slippery, slimy, scaly skin come another group.
How many eyes do they have? You may query,
About ten, no, five, no, one,
Many shapes and sizes may they come in,
Many colours and numbers.
All these monsters are equally horrifying,
They are hiding in every dark corner,

Some even in plain sight.
So be careful where you step tonight,
Because they might just choose you!

Poppy Phillpotts (9)
Pilling St John's CE School, Pilling

My Friendly Monster

When I'm feeling low and very sad,
I close my eyes to escape,
And there is my friendly monster, Glad Brad,
With his great big smiling face.

With big, wide arms to greet me,
Giving a warm, imaginary hug,
He sits and listens to my worries,
My room transformed into a happy monster's snug.

He dances around, pulling funny faces,
"You're so funny, Glad Brad, I love you so much,"
And, as I open my eyes, he fades into the distance,
But I know my magic monster will stay in touch.

So it's good to have a friendly monster,
As, in life, not everything is as it seems,
So give a chance to the beast as well as beauty,
They could turn out to be the one in your dreams.

Hannah Wilson (10)
Pilling St John's CE School, Pilling

Teddy

Lying there, silent and still, over the end of my bed,
All cute and cuddly, a thought of a monster wouldn't run through my head.
By day, he is known as Ted,
With soft, fluffy fur that makes cuddles so warm,
He would make a perfect gift for a newborn.
But as the day closes, Ted's not looking like roses,
In fact, toy Ted is turning into ferocious Fred.
His blazing red eyes search the room for his prize,
His vicious clawed fingers wrapped around rosy skin,
Clutching hold, tight, to the prize he must win.
Looming large, the end must be near,
His colossal yellow horns are a sight to fear.
But what's that smile? He wasn't so vile,
He was gripping onto Riley's doll for a while.

Elizabeth Hill (10)
Pilling St John's CE School, Pilling

The Snortecdra

Don't you get annoyed about those pesky little mice
As they scamper around in the street,
Crawling in the alleyway, along with the lice?
But wait, hang on a minute...
Who on Earth do those beady eyes belong to
Hiding in the shadows on such a dark night?
And, who does have a trumpet-like nose?
All of those gnarly teeth, gleaming in the dim street light,
Where did all the mice go?
Where are all the lice?
Sucked up in one big gulp,
A deep voice mumbling, "Nice."
Slithering out of the darkness,
All of the mysteries clicked into place,
Because when the Snortecdra is about,
You'd better run and hide your face!

Geno Gamble (10)
Stalham Academy, Stalham

The Monster In My Park

I can smell a disgusting beast,
It can see me as its feast,
I can hear a vile growl,
It sounds like a beast on the prowl,
It's pacing up and down in the dark,
What is this creature in my park?

I crept up close to get near,
I moved closer to his pointy ear,
I carefully reached out and stroked his fur,
He must have liked it, he gave the loudest purr,
Rolling around on his back with his belly in the air,
Suddenly, I wasn't scared, I didn't have a care.

Isla Smithson (9)
Stalham Academy, Stalham

The Sound Of The Sniffles

As I sleep, the floorboards creak,
Down in the basement,
Where nobody goes,
The sound in my ear,
Of a sniffling nose.

I hide under the covers, trembling in fear,
The sound of the sniffles seems frightfully near,
I creep downstairs,
"Is anybody there?" I whisper softly,
But all I hear is the sound of the sniffles.

Into the basement, where nobody goes,
The sound in my ear,
Of a sniffling nose,
"Is anybody there?" I say again,
But once more, all I can hear is the sound of the sniffles.

I peek around the corner only to see
A giant fluff-ball sitting before me,
I take a step forward and sit down beside him,

His fluffy fur rubs against my cheek and I suddenly realise,
The sound of the sniffles is coming from him!

He doesn't have hayfever, nor a cold,
But is crying his eyes out, what is about to unfold?
I give him a hug and he calms down immediately,
"All I want is a friend, but everybody's scared of me!"

Olivia Kelly (10)
Stanton Road Primary School, Bebington

When I Go To Sleep

When I go to sleep,
I hear the floorboards creak,
My eyes open in a flash,
Bigger than an owl's,
Brighter than a lantern on a starless night,
Then I see a glowing light, fading quickly.

When I go back to sleep,
I hear the floorboards creak,
I see it,
It has midnight scales,
Glowing extendable nails,
And a great, big, swishing tail.

As I sleep,
I hear the floorboards creak,
It has glowing eyes like lava,
Wings that could send a deadly breeze,
Nostrils so big, they looked like black holes,
And teeth as sharp as razors.

Then with an explosion of fire,
And a scraping of claws,
Silence floods the room.

No one knows what happened that day,
No one will ever know what happened that day,
All we know is that the floorboards no longer
creeaak...

Elodie Casey (10)
Stanton Road Primary School, Bebington

Beady-Eyed Beast

This three-eyed crawly
Has needle-like teeth,
Devilish red eyes,
And an appetite for naughty children!

It could gobble you up in seconds,
Eat you alive and leave you in crumbs,
It creeps and crawls around at night,
Hunting for its mouth-watering prey.

Its oval-shaped head is not just hideous, but monumental,
Its furry body looks fluffy, but could injure you in seconds,
You could be left in pieces from being a victim of this monster,
Beware, and stay alert for it could be life-threatening.

It lives in the deepest, darkest hole, where no one goes,
It's unknown how it lives but it's certain it lives in a hole,

Its lair is equipped with high-tech traps,
This destroyer could attack you at any moment...

Louie Jones (10)
Stanton Road Primary School, Bebington

Levi The Monster

L urking in the shadows
E veryone was petrified
V iciously attacking everybody in his way
I magine if he catches me!

T onight is the most terrifying night of my life
H e's got razor-sharp teeth, as sharp as a knife
E ven his eyes make you tremble with fear

M onstrous horns, like an evil devil
O h no, my best friend is getting chased by the horrifying creature!
N ooo! *Gobble, gobble, gobble*
S ilently creeping away, so this terrible monster doesn't eat me
T hank goodness, it was a dream
E verybody is safe!
R emember, nightmares are not real.

Billy (10)
Stanton Road Primary School, Bebington

Ozzy Under My Bed

I saw a monster under my bed,
It creaks on the floorboards when I'm asleep,
Its glowing white eyes make kids scream,
You can see its fur glow gold.

But I can smell its sweet breath and it calms me,
Its soft fur which makes me sleepy,
Its tender eyes look caringly at me,
Then, I said, "Hello."

It jumped back in surprise,
It said, "'Ello little girl,"
I smiled, it felt like the first time,
It then spoke again, "I'm Ozzy the dream-monster."

Ozzy and I had adventures in the moonlight,
I went to Monster Dreamland,
Then I grew older, we had to say goodbye.

Bethan Barnes (10)
Stanton Road Primary School, Bebington

Is There A Monster In My House?

I can hear the sound of the fridge.
I hope I am dreaming, I think to myself.
Is that the noise of a giant stomping?
What am I going to do if it comes into my room?

A giant vicious beast is in my home.
What if I go down there and it attacks me?
Should I stay up here and carry on being scared
Or should I go down there and confront the beast?

I finally worked up the courage to go down there.
The monster was cute and friendly, it didn't attack me.
I edged forward and stroked the monster.
I think it liked me.

Unfortunately, it was all an amazing dream.

Luke Brockway (10)
Stanton Road Primary School, Bebington

Treecer The Scary Monster

Treecer, the tree-monster,
Was very scary and big,
With his long, sharp tongue,
And his massive teeth,
A big horn on his head.

But really, Treecer was just lonely,
See, being big and scary makes you grumpy,
Maybe if he had a friend, he'd be fine,
Because he's gentle and kind,
As well as fluffy and soft to hug.

One day, a little boy sees him,
The little boy wasn't scared,
So he ran to him, and gave him a big hug,
He felt his fluffy, soft body,
And said, "Will you be my friend?"

Charlie Jeakins (10)
Stanton Road Primary School, Bebington

Trouble On Halloween!

What do you mean,
You've never seen
A monster that is very keen
To destroy people's houses,
That are very clean,
On Halloween?

But, once he's done it,
He is very quick,
And pretends he's having a picnic,
"A picnic, you say, that sounds nice,"
But the mess he makes
Will ruin your day.

He's very small,
Purple and green,
And the biggest mouth you've ever seen,
But when he gets caught,
He tells a lie,
And a minute later, he starts to fly!

Olivia Hanrahan (10)
Stanton Road Primary School, Bebington

Mythical Monster

You're telling me you have never heard of a monster?
Well, that is about to change,
You see, some can be nice,
On the other hand, some are gruesome,
And if you encounter one be brave,
Because the one thing they love most is fear!

So here's a tip, you must remember,
Be brave and save everyone,
Watch your back,
You never know, they might attack,
When night falls,
Their fangs grow sharp,
So stay alert,
And fight back.
Good luck,
You'll need it.

Fenja Doolan (10)
Stanton Road Primary School, Bebington

Ox Puket That's The Name

Under the floorboards of Ground Street, in every house,
Heard scratching and a loud noise,
No one knew why or how,
Because everyone was way too scared to look under the floor.
'Til one day and one man found a monster!
He named him Ox Puket,
Because the man's name was Sam Puket,
And the monster's eyes were in the shape of an ox.
The monster came out,
Everyone had peace and quiet,
But no one knows that he can scare, fright and maybe even do something terrible...
Kill!

Eva Phillips (10)
Stanton Road Primary School, Bebington

Monster Walk

Early we were walking, with the dog on lead tight,
As we bounded along the coastal path,
Nearly home, with a sea breeze to enjoy, as the sun rose.

The bushes separated and, as slow as an elephant, an obese beast appeared,
A purposeful, pounding, plodding, lumbering, flea-ridden monster.

Then Bertie (the dog) started to attack, as he swallowed my friend,
He walked away, leaving his putrid smell in the air,
My blood curdled as he left the area, where I stood stock-still.

Douglas Waters (10)
Stanton Road Primary School, Bebington

Just A Dream

One late night, in my dark and damp bedroom,
Something slowly crept up the creaky stairs,
Something scary? Something mysterious?

Leaping under the covers in a flash,
Something touched my shoulder!
In a shock, I glanced over my cover,
And saw a giant, one-eyed, green monster.

Hairy, green and with one big eye,
It made me quiver and it almost made me cry,
Why do I dream of such horrible things?
What a relief, the alarm clock rings. Phew!

Thomas Harris (10)
Stanton Road Primary School, Bebington

The Night Of The Living Pumpkin

We made the pumpkin for Halloween,
But he wasn't meant to be this mean.
We made him from a pumpkin,
And he made me jump out of my skin.

He came alive and flew around,
And made people dive on the ground,
I heard them all shout and scream,
So I decided to intervene.

I smashed him up and chopped him down,
And that got rid of his stupid frown.
Next year, I think I will stay in bed,
So that I can avoid the living dead.

Daniel Skinner (11)
Stanton Road Primary School, Bebington

I Am...
(Inspired by This is Halloween by Danny Elfman)

I am the one who's hiding under the bed,
Teeth so sharp and eyes glowing red.
I am the who when you call 'Who's there?'
A whisper in the wind and then a scare.
I am the one who makes the floorboards creak,
Then, when you see me, I hear you shriek.
I am the one floating swiftly through the air,
Turning it to ice so I can scare.
I am the feeling of someone watching you,
You can't escape me, even if you dare.

Maya Khan (10)
Stanton Road Primary School, Bebington

The Monster Under My Bed

The moonlit sky creeping in,
My door gaping open,
The gentle breeze swaying the curtain,
Stairs creaking outside my door.

Then, a noise came from under my bed,
A bright beam of light,
Two wiry lines sticking out of the edge of the bed.

Then, out came a nerve-chilling monster,
A bright beaming eye,
Long, thin antennae,
And pencil-like teeth,
Razor-sharp claws can sever anything in its way.

Calum Smith (10)
Stanton Road Primary School, Bebington

Monsters!

Bob and his friend, playing hide-and-seek,
The leaves shivering in fear,
The buzzing of bees is gone, like there is no one left in the world,
The giant monster lurking out to get me,
Bob causing mischief wherever he goes,
His snake-like skin is made of rough scales,
Oh no, there is something under my bed,
I hope it's not...

Alice Matchett (10)
Stanton Road Primary School, Bebington

Bobby's Hobby

Bobby has only one hobby,
Which is scaring Robbie.
Bobby is a slimy, whiny, fish-devil,
He wears a huge glass helmet,
With gross, green pond-water in it.
Luckily, Robbie has only one hobby,
Which is scaring Bobby,
Who lives under his bed,
And always bumps his head!

Elly Noone (11)
Stanton Road Primary School, Bebington

The Cute Monster In Your Closet

Heidi is the monster in your closet,
Tiptoeing up those stairs,
She's cold, snuggly and wants a hug,
Are you cuddling her? What a surprise,
A shame she doesn't have human eyes,
While you are all snug in your bed,
You hear her creeping...
Boo!

Rosie Mae Higginson (10)
Stanton Road Primary School, Bebington

YOUNG WRITERS INFORMATION

We hope you have enjoyed reading this book – and that you will continue to in the coming years.

If you're a young writer who enjoys reading and creative writing, or the parent of an enthusiastic poet or story writer, do visit our website www.youngwriters.co.uk. Here you will find free competitions, workshops and games, as well as recommended reads, a poetry glossary and our blog. There's lots to keep budding writers motivated to write!

If you would like to order further copies of this book, or any of our other titles, then please give us a call or order via your online account.

Young Writers
Remus House
Coltsfoot Drive
Peterborough
PE2 9BF
(01733) 890066
info@youngwriters.co.uk

Join in the conversation!
Tips, news, giveaways and much more!

f YoungWritersUK **y** @YoungWritersCW